How to S] in 10 Simple Steps

The Ultimate Guide for Transforming You into a Speed-Reading Machine

Richard Banks

Thank You!

Thank you for your purchase.

I am dedicated to making the most enriching and informational content. I hope it meets your expectations and you gain a lot from it.

Your comments and feedback are important to me because they help me to provide the best material possible. So, if you have any questions or concerns, please email me at richardbanks.books@gmail.com.

Again, thank you for your purchase.

INTRODUCTION

As a person enormously inspired by Warren Buffet, I've always been intrigued to learn more about his habits, interests, and ideas. Whether watching documentaries about him, subscribing to his online talks, or reading about Berkshire Hathaway, as I learned about his accomplishments, I did everything I could to understand how he was able to achieve so much over the years.

One day, I came across a documentary that depicted Buffet's life and accomplishments. He was asked about the keys to success, and he said, "Read 500 pages every day. That's how knowledge works. It builds up like compound interest. All of you can do it, but I guarantee not many of you will do it."

This piece of knowledge struck me like a lightning bolt. How did I not know this, and why was I not implementing this strategy? With no other thought in mind, I ordered five books from Amazon about subjects I'd always been interested in. I couldn't contain my excitement to delve deeply into these books.

The books arrived, and I threw myself into them. I read a couple of pages with keen interest until I realized that I was constantly re-reading previous paragraphs. New knowledge was unveiling itself before me, but what was up *with* me? Why did I feel a strong urge to go back, skim previous pages, and make sure I knew what the author was trying to convey? Why couldn't I grasp the concepts during my first reading of the material?

The frustration grew stronger. With each page and every word that appeared before my eyes, a growing contempt for books poured out of me. No matter how much I wanted to read books that grabbed my interest, my excitement continued to diminish. I started to move away from books and questioned the primary underlying purpose in doing so. It seemed to me there was no point in reading unless you could absorb the information and make a difference in your life.

Time went by until, one day, I searched online for "effective reading." Multiple links appeared, most of which consisted of online platforms where people from diverse communities shared their experience in reading books. Although there were people who spoke of their resentment toward reading, I also discovered many people who said they truly appreciated their reading skills and encouraged others to improve theirs. That's where I found it wasn't just me; many people struggled to get a handle on reading. At the same time, some people raved about the advantages of being able to read effectively.

Amongst the plethora of comments on the webpage, I saw a link to an article titled "The Guide to Speed Reading." As I skimmed through the lines, the words felt more and more relatable, as if the article was written specifically for me. That day, my approach to reading changed. After getting to know the concept of speed reading, how it works, and how it helps, I've finished dozens of books while retaining the information in them.

If you also go through any of the above challenges, allow me to take you on a journey of self-realization and, eventually, to a stage where you'll be able to read up to 100 books in a year. The techniques taught in this book will at least double your reading rate and learning speed in just one week. We'll explore the root causes of why we remain stuck on one page—unable to move forward with satisfaction—and delve deeply into techniques that allow us to be active and efficient readers.

How to Speed Read in 10 Simple Steps is an easy, step-by-step guide in which you'll discover the history of reading, assess your current reading level, and pinpoint areas you need to improve on. Then, we'll explore the 10 simple steps to speed read and retain loads of information.

The concept, methods, and applications of reading efficiently have come a long way over recent decades. With new advancements, research, and application of knowledge, the world of science has come out with enormous changes and benefits in many areas, including reading. Compared to what reading looked like in the Middle Ages and even before that, the scope of possibilities available through reading has vastly expanded. The essence of this book is to explore the diversity of reading, how it evolved over the years, how it's done today, and, most importantly, what can be done to increase your reading speed.

The process of speed reading is founded on the reader recognizing sentences as a whole rather than taking in each word and absorbing it. This allows the reader to comprehend entire sentences and grasp their meaning much faster. The rate at which an average person reads is about 200-250 words per minute; however, speed reading will boost your speed, giving you the potential to read 500 words per minute. To achieve this skill, dedication, effort, and persistence are required

Almost everyone on the planet is living a hectic life today. Whether it's being in middle school and turning in assignments or running a business while juggling responsibilities at home, everyone struggles to find time for themselves just to enjoy a hot cup of coffee, let alone have a dedicated hour or two to read a book. Nevertheless, the passion for reading books remains high. Everyone wants to read books of interest to them, learn from them, and implement that knowledge in their lives. What they lack is the focused time required to do it.

Keeping this perspective in mind, this book aims to cater to all those who don't have enough time and yet want to retain information quicker and more easily. This book is for those who live a busy life and yet want to put in the effort required to learn about speed reading and reap its benefits. Students who lack proper comprehension while reading and face difficulties preserving information in their brains can benefit from this book and do better in their classes. Adults who are determined to learn and apply this knowledge in their everyday lives are also encouraged to give this a read.

After reading this book, I promise you'll be able to double or triple your reading speed so you can save at least an hour a day in reading time. (That's 365 hours per year!)

At first, it may seem that you can't retain anything using the process of speed reading. However, with continuous practice and the right motivation, you'll develop a sense of confidence, obtain better problem-solving skills, and enhance your leadership qualities. You'll also feel a sense of empowerment in your social circle because this book will improve your speaking and comprehension skills.

CHAPTER 1 - LET'S GET STARTED

"A reader lives a thousand lives before he dies. The man who never reads lives only one." -George R.R. Martin

The Benefits of Reading

Theory of Mind

Reading provides us with enormous benefits. Through reading, we acquire an ability known as "theory of mind," which involves learning specific skills that help us to be more sociable, whatever our surroundings. Such skills can be established in children when they read about fictional characters and relate to their situations. For example, a short story for kids may instill the fundamental virtues of empathy, kindness, and affection for others.

Expanded Vocabulary

It's an almost undeniable fact that reading increases our vocabulary. It exposes us to different cultures, stories, and lives depending on the context of what we're reading and pushes us to learn new words, new phrases, and proverbs. For instance, whenever a child comes across a new word—for example, "significant"— he asks his parents or teacher what it means. This habit of finding new words and learning their meaning enables us to read advanced research papers when we're older.

Enhanced Cognitive Functioning

The National Institute of Aging promotes reading at all levels because research shows that people actively engaged in reading and solving puzzles have better cognitive functioning and display milder symptoms of neurological disorders in old age compared to those who don't participate in these activities during their lives.

Alleviation of Stress

Reading has also been scientifically proven to reduce stress, along with other mindful activities such as yoga or humor. Incorporating reading for 30 minutes into your daily routine takes your mind off stressful thoughts and promotes mental well-being.

Sleep Improvement

Reading stimulates better sleep. It's often considered the best activity to adopt before going to bed because it slows your heart rate, lowers blood pressure, and enhances your body's equilibrium.

Reading Practices in Childhood

There are no bad readers, just those with bad reading habits. We didn't learn how to read efficiently when we were growing up. Chances are, from the moment you were first taught how to read, you were taught inept reading strategies. We were all trained to read slowly in elementary school. Once you learn proper reading techniques and turn your new reading behaviors into a habit, reading faster will become effortless. Instilling the habit of reading early on in childhood helps accelerate a child's reading skills and better prepare them to make a living as adults, because most jobs require basic reading skills. From the beginning, if parents are successful in building a positive association between books and their children, their children will grow up to be fast readers.

Split and Read

Our parents and teachers used various techniques to teach us to read when we were young. One of the most well-known ways is to split a word into its two or three components (syllables) and join them together gradually to eventually pronounce the word—for example, initially breaking the word "banana" into "ba-na-na" to make it easier to see the components of the word and pronounce them.

Vocalization

Another method actively used by parents and teachers to teach children to pronounce words correctly is to have them read the words aloud to promote speaking them and also so any mispronounced words can be corrcctcd.

Use of Pictures

Using pictures is a helpful—although somewhat time-consuming—way to teach a child to read and provide them with entertainment. Visual aids allow their imagination to assist in learning words. The use of pictures broadens their creativity and can supplement the learning of complex words.

Talk about What They're Reading

Parents can reinforce their child's imagination by allowing them to speak about what they read.

****

These techniques can be valuable tools when encouraging a child to read; however, if adhered to for a long time during a child's development, they may lead to poor reading habits in the long run.

Since time and dedication are required to learn to read in childhood, it's okay to use the aforementioned techniques to make word comprehension and pronunciation easier. However, if an adult reads a book by vocalizing every word, this greatly slows down his reading time.

Problems arise not when we use such techniques but rather when we don't grow out of them over time. If we realize we need to boost our reading skills and let go of the kindergarten practices we used as a child, we'll be able to explore new horizons in reading.

How To Self-Motivate Yourself to Read and Get Through This Book

Be Clear About Your Purpose

When deciding to read a particular book, always be clear about why you chose it. You should never force yourself to do something you're not interested in. Have a pre-defined purpose for every book you get your hands on.

Set Personalized Goals and Stay Dedicated

Setting goals for yourself and associating deadlines with them will help you achieve your objectives and keep your reading routine on a designated path (Yong Kang Chan, 2021).

Dedication will push you through the hard times and assure that you make it through the entire process.

Remove Distractions

One of the most significant steps before attempting to read any book—whether it be coursework, fiction, a memoir, or the one you're reading right now—is to make sure you have no distractions. Distractions can include a constantly ringing phone, people texting you, a noisy environment, or having a to-do list dancing in your head while you try to read. Silence your phone, find a place to read in which you'll be undisturbed, and dedicate yourself to the pleasant experience of reading a book.

Be Comfortable

You'll never be able to immerse yourself in the true essence of reading unless you're sitting at ease. Make sure you're physically comfortable with no disturbing thoughts. Your consciousness should be fully present when you're reading a book, so invest the time and attention necessary to grasp the essence of what you're reading rather than being distracted by an uncomfortable chair or dwelling on a worry or fantasy.

Take Breaks

No matter what kind of a book you're putting your attention onto, always take breaks after reading four to five pages. The break doesn't have to be long, but it should ensure that you're fully present when you resume reading. Another benefit of taking a break is that it gives you time to ponder what you just read. It could be a philosophical thought that comes to mind or maybe an emotion that you wouldn't have noticed if you'd not taken a break.

Write About It

To make sure you're fully grasping the idea of a book, keep a paper and pencil with you. Draw, write, or even scribble a note about whatever comes to your mind after reading a chapter or a section. This will help you reflect on and absorb what you just read.

Assess Your Level of Reading

Before discussing speed-reading techniques, it's necessary to first assess your current reading rate so a thorough analysis can be done after using the speed-reading techniques. You must establish your baseline reading rate and retention of information so these can be compared later on with the results after you've learned how to speed read.

Reading Level Test

For this activity, you'll need:

- A book to read to test yourself – preferably one that you haven't read before.
- A stopwatch or timer (you can use the one on your phone). Set the timer for two minutes.
- Pen or pencil.
- Sheet of paper to make notes.
- Spreadsheet to keep a record of your progress.

After setting the timer for two minutes, start reading from your chosen book. When the timer goes off, mark where you stopped on the page.

Next, grab the paper and pencil at your side and start writing down everything you can remember about what you just read without referring to the book. This doesn't have to be the exact words, but it should carry the same meaning. This acts as a measure of how well you retain information after reading.

The next step is to calculate the words per minute (WPM). For that, the formula is:

$$\frac{\text{The average number of words per line} \times \text{total number of lines read}}{\text{time (mins)}}$$

For instance, if there's an average of 16 words per line, and you were able to read 20 lines, you multiply 16 times 20 and then divide that total by 2 (the number of minutes):

$$16 \times 20 = 320$$
$$320/2 = 160 \text{ WPM}$$

To further evaluate your reading level, refer to the WPM scale below:

WPM Scale

- WPM less than 120: Below-average reader
- WPM between 120-180: Below average for adults

- WPM between 180-240: Average reader
- WPM between 240-350: Average college level
- WPM between 350-500: Above average
- WPM above 500: Superior reader

Using the example above, the reading rate of 160 WPM is below average for adults. For self-analysis, continuously repeat the test and track your progress as you go through the book.

CHAPTER 2: WHAT IS SPEED READING?

According to the website, mindtools.org, speed reading refers to a reading capability that involves quick recognition and comprehension of words, sentences, phrases, or even entire paragraphs all at once, which results in enhanced reading speed (words per minute).

As the amount of content to be grasped increases day by day—be it news, emails, or even recipes—the skill of speed reading allows you to maximize your time to accommodate your lifestyle and routine.

Understanding How Your Brain Works to Achieve Speed Reading

Neuroplasticity

Neuroplasticity is the brain's ability to form connections. These connections can be as simple as connecting the stimulus of touching a hot pan with the realization of pain or as complex as building an algorithm. Neuroplasticity comes into play whenever the brain forms deep neural pathways, including those initiated by receptors for hearing, sight, or touch.

The same concept is applied to reading. The more you read, the deeper the connections in the brain that relate to vocabulary, comprehension, and reading rate.

In a study conducted at the Max Planck Institute for Psycholinguistics in the Netherlands, a group of women over the age of 30 were taught to read. During the first six months, these previously illiterate women had the same reading skills as that of a first-grader. Brain scans were taken before, during, and after the

28

completion of the experiment. When the brain scans were analyzed, the results showed that each subject's brain structure vastly changed during this period.

This change was the result of neuroplasticity, the ability of the brain to rewire itself. The outer layer—the cortex—changes its structure, and the deep inner areas of the brain stem and thalamus alter their anatomy to be in sync with the changes in the outer layer. Similarly, as the brain acquires new information during the process of reading, its outer and inner structures change.

Human Memory

The human brain works almost like a muscle whenever we begin to acquire new information, whether it's learning a new subject, memorizing lyrics of a song, or trying to remember the ingredients of a recipe. Just like we strengthen our muscles by working out regularly, we need to adopt the same habit when using our brains.

You've most likely witnessed the effects of lethargy when you open your school books after months of ignoring them. You can't concentrate for even 10 minutes. It seems everything in your life presses in to distract you, and you aren't motivated to stick with your studies. Just like your muscles fatigue easily after you haven't exercised for months, and your body aches terribly the day after you resume your exercise routine, your brain is initially inflexible when it comes to taking in new information. Therefore, you need to maintain a routine of active reading, so your brain is more easily able to acquire new knowledge and function smoothly in the process.

Speed-Reading Benefits

Improves Memory

As discussed earlier, using your brain efficiently to read faster than you previously did boosts your memory and helps you retain more information in less time. With the help of speed reading, you'll be able to read a plethora of content, intake a multitude of knowledge, and be able to organize material effectively.

Enhances Logical Thinking

Logic is the process of connecting the dots as you continue to gain knowledge—combining previous information with newer information to build full explanations in your brain. For instance, a logical argument can be made from the realization that you suffered from nausea as a side effect when you were on an antibiotic and no longer experienced nausea when the course of the antibiotic ended. Logic suggests that the antibiotic caused the nausea. A simplistic form of logic is when you can connect one situation with another and develop a plausible explanation.

When you speed read, your brain becomes a pro at making correlations because it has a lot of information that it can categorize and use to build associations.

Saves Time

One of the most common reasons people want to learn to speed read is that they want to keep up with daily happenings in the world, learn new information, or enjoy a best-selling spy thriller and save time doing it. Reading faster allows you to consume more knowledge in significantly less time by using techniques that have been researched and practiced for years.

Uses a Focused-Goals Approach

By using speed-reading techniques, you focus on specific keywords and read the sentence as a whole rather than splitting it into components. Your approach will be focused, and you'll dedicate your time to achieving your reading goals.

Enhances Productivity

Shortening the time required to obtain and retain information results in increased productivity. There will be no time wasted, no lack of concentration, and you'll actually enjoy any reading chore that you're faced with.

Reduces Eye Strain

Speed reading is all about working smarter rather than working harder. Working smartly allows you to save time, stay focused, and get the job done in a shorter time, and it also is more restful for your eyes.

Promotes Emotional Well-Being

Active meditation is defined as a state of mind achieved by doing a task with complete focus and immersion. When using speed-reading techniques, you'll become deeply engrossed in the content you're reading and not be subject to external distractions. The process reduces stress and promotes emotional well-being.

Enhances Sociability

When you're good at retaining concepts, logical explanations, or general information, you can excel in conversation by bringing up exciting topics and facts.

Speed-Reading Misconceptions

Warren Buffet, CEO of Berkshire Hathaway, claims to have a routine of reading 600 to 1,000 pages per day. Think about this for a minute. A business magnate like Buffet must need seven to eight hours to do this much reading daily. If so, how does he get the time to focus on investing in businesses, working as a philanthropist, and maintaining a work-life balance?

Well, you guessed it—he's a speed reader! He doesn't need hours to do all that reading, which means he has time for all his other duties. He's reaping the benefits of a skill he learned years ago and has maintained to the present day.

You may have some preconceived ideas about what speed reading is, and you may have heard mixed reviews about how helpful it is. Let's separate fact from fiction by exploring the common misconceptions about speed reading.

1. Reading More than 500 WPM Is Impossible!

Studies have shown that, on average, high-level executives read more than 575 WPM, and college professors read 675 WPM. Anne Jones, a world-renowned avid reader, holds the speed-reading record: 4,700 words per minute with a comprehension level of 67%. We mention these facts to make you aware that reading more than 500 words per minute isn't an extraordinary feat that's only been achieved by a few gifted readers. Reading at this rate is doable, and almost anyone can learn to read even 1,000 words per minute.

2. You Skip Words when You Speed Read

Although your cyes don't fixate on every word in a sentence when you speed read, you still absorb the content. The process involves reading words in groups to make sense of the entire sentence.

3. You Enjoy Reading Less when You Speed Read

Many readers claim you won't enjoy a book as much if you read it fast as you would by taking your time and focusing on every word. This is a total myth. The degree of enjoyment doesn't depend on how fast or slow you read. It depends on how well you comprehend the meaning of what you're reading. A passionate reader may enjoy a book reading at a rate of 1,050 WPM, and a beginner may not find pleasure even in reading 150 words per minute.

4. Learning to Speed Read Is Expensive

Many people think that since speed reading has become so popular, and almost everyone is talking about how they're benefitting from it, it must be for super-rich folks. It seems it must cost a lot of money to learn a skill that's so highly rated, but that's not correct. In every aspect of learning, what matters is your approach and your attitude toward learning.

It's critical to always keep in mind that there's no limit to what you can learn. There are always multiple opportunities and paths for individuals to learn in today's society, but you must be motivated and dedicated to educating yourself. Being committed to something means you're willing to make sacrifices and create the necessary time to reach your goals.

5. Speed Reading Diminishes your Memory and Retention

Research shows that if you purposely read slowly in the hope of enhancing your retention, this makes it easier to become distracted and start daydreaming. If you intentionally read slowly, your brain is naturally drawn to whatever is happening around you that seems more exciting. The opposite of this myth—that reading slowly improves retention—is actually the case. Not only does speed reading improve your memory, but it also trains your brain, so your retention and comprehension are better.

6. Everyone Has a Natural Reading Speed

Everyone has a particular potential for learning new skills, be it drawing, reading, or driving. The ability to read is acquired through a designed learning process that commences when you're a toddler. Regular practice and training help you become a good reader. The amount of reading experience you have and the techniques you've developed over the years dictate your reading level.

Speed-Reading Limitations

It's Not Helpful for Critics

While a reader's motive for reading a book is to get to the gist and learn from it, a critic's motive isn't quite the same. By critic, I mean not only those people who evaluate a book but also debutante writers who are getting into the world of authors and trying to learn from their writing. These are new writers focusing on the author's choice of words, sentence cadence, use of dialogue, and emotion. All these things can't be evaluated using speed-reading techniques, as the motive here is different.

It's More Work

When you speed read, your eyes are focused on looking for specific words that are key to getting at the gist of the book. You pay more and more attention to what your eyes just took in, and your brain is constantly in alert mode. You aren't given time to sit back, relax, and think about what you read or contemplate its implications. Because of all these factors, speed reading can be pretty exhausting at times.

When you speed read, it's more of a task than a hobby. You may find yourself tired after doing 30 minutes of speed reading; however, your stamina will undoubtedly improve with time. Once you do that, it won't seem like much of a hassle.

Limitations of the Eye

One of the most significant limitations of speed reading is the efficiency of your eyes when reading. The concept of speed reading came into existence mainly when the idea of eye fixation was discovered. Let's look at this in detail.

Eye fixation refers to the minute pause that occurs in the motion of your eyes when you're reading a sentence, cooking a dish, or driving a car. It's that split-second of time in which your eyes fixate themselves on a particular object, word, on any other tangible thing, grasp its content and meaning, and then move on to the next word or object on which your eyes fixate for another brief moment.

Consider this example: You're out in the woods, roaming around in a National Park, and taking in the scenery. Note that even though the whole scene is before you, your eyes don't fixate themselves on each object. They may pause for a moment if you think you see a deer and then move on to look at the sky and fixate for a moment on the grey clouds above you. The point here is that, for any specific content to register in your brain, your eyes need to fixate, move, on and then fixate again.

Such is the process of reading. Your eyes fixate on each and every word, comprehend its meaning, and then move on. Hearing this, you may think the human eye must need a lot of time to fixate itself on one word, understand it, and then move to the next. However, this isn't the case; the average eye-fixation period only lasts from 50 milliseconds to 600 milliseconds.

However, even though fixation happens this quickly, it still serves as a physiological limitation in the process of speed reading. Though this natural process of eye fixation can't be altered, the timespan of each eye fixation can be significantly reduced so that large amounts of content are grasped within one instant of focus. This is, in fact, the basis of speed reading—to minimize the duration of each fixation.

Three things are directly linked to eye fixation and influence your reading speed: vision span, vocabulary, and subject familiarity.

Eye Fixation and Vision Span

Also known as peripheral vision, vision span is the range of text available to the eye in one fixation. For instance, if you're a beginner at reading and are capable of reading two words in one fixation, you have a relatively narrow vision span. Assuming that a complete sentence consists of 16 words, it will take you eight fixations to read one sentence. Further, presuming that one of your fixations takes your 400 milliseconds, it will take you 3.2 seconds to read one sentence. Now, that's certainly not a good speed when you're trying to read at a faster pace.

With this understanding of the concept of vision span, it makes sense that fast readers have broad vision spans and, eventually, fewer eye fixations. By using speed-reading techniques and trying to read a sentence as a whole without fixating your eyes on each word, you can achieve one fixation per sentence. Now, compare that to your previous eight fixations per second and notice the difference in speed. Excellent, right?

Eye Fixation and Vocabulary

Read this sentence to understand the relationship of vocabulary to eye fixation:

"Owls and Yead win the race."

It probably took you four to five fixations to read this sentence and, after that, you may not have been able to derive its meaning. This is because the vocabulary is confusing. To reveal the secret, the sentence above is a jumbled form of the famous English idiom, "Slow and steady wins the race." Because two of the six words in this sentence are scrambled, you had to focus more, eventually maximizing your fixation to make sense of what you're reading.

With an expanding vocabulary comes greater understanding. When you know more words, your eyes won't have to fixate on each word in the sentence; they'll simply register the word and move on. However, the smaller your vocabulary, the smaller your vision span. It's like when we encounter a new shop and stop to study it to learn more about it.

To increase your vocabulary, you can make good use of that dusty and long-neglected dictionary on your shelf. Make a habit of learning a few new words per day, and check the next day to make sure you retained their meaning.

You can create a ritual of using a "Word of the Day Calendar" to write the particular word you learned the meaning of that day on the calendar. It will be quite an achievement when, at the end of the year, you have 365 new words in your memory and, of course, on your calendar.

Games such as Scrabble and Word Jumble can also be helpful not only to learn new words but also to discover words you never guessed existed.

Eye Fixation and Subject Familiarity

If you are *not* a medical student or a practitioner, this sentence is a perfect example of the importance of subject familiarity: "Lymph nodes are small oval bodies of the lymphatic system that act as filters, with an internal honeycomb of connective tissue filled with lymphocytes and macrophages that collect and destroy bacteria, viruses, and foreign matter from lymph." (Lymph Node, 2021)

The familiarity you have with the topic you're trying to speed read serves as the most significant contributor to your pace. If you're like me, you're not a medical student, so the sentence above is challenging to comprehend and may take you more fixations as compared to reading about topics you're familiar with.

What you can do is read about topics under various headings such as politics, history, archaeology, and whatnot to increase your knowledge span. This will improve not only your reading speed but also your IQ level.

Speed Reading vs. Comprehension

In recent times, at least a few research studies have been conducted to test the results of speed reading and its influence on comprehending the meaning of what's being read. The most important fact that's been discovered in a limited number of studies—i.e., not yet made public and not widely known—is that the rate of reading doesn't have a drastic impact on the comprehension ability of the reader.

In one experiment, half the students were asked to read at a slower pace, while the other half were encouraged to read rapidly. As the students followed the guidelines given to them and began reading about their respective subjects, certain factors were

44

evaluated. These factors included eye movement, body posture, and concentration, all of which were observed in real time. However, to the researchers' surprise, the results weren't as anticipated.

The data showed there was little correspondence between the rate of speed reading and the level of comprehension. Further, it was found that the students who were asked to read slowly showed diminished comprehension, and the non-verbal cues observed while they were reading weren't as focused as those of the other group in the experiment. On the other hand, the students who were motivated to read faster displayed higher levels of comprehension and a better attitude about the task.

The main takeaway from this study is that comprehension depends on the ability of readers to pay attention to the specific and most important details of a topic. Once they're able to do that, it becomes easier for them to focus on certain lines and paragraphs and skip the rest. This activity enhances comprehension, and speed reading supports this.

When juggling reading rate and comprehension, there are two likely possibilities: one, that reading fluency is better than comprehension or, two, comprehension is much better than reading accuracy.

With the first possibility—when reading fluency is better—the task is to work on your comprehension skills. To do this, try stopping yourself after a few lines and ask yourself specific and closed-ended questions regarding what you just read. For instance, if you've just read a few pages of a novel, ask yourself questions like:

- What are the names of the characters in this passage?
- Can I describe the environment around them?
- How do they seem to be interacting with their environment?
- What happened in the paragraph I just read?

Including this exercise regularly in your reading routine will force you to make this a habit, and you'll remember to look for specific details in whatever material you're reading. The foundation of speed reading is to strengthen the reader's capacity to make wise decisions about what should be skimmed, skipped, and thoroughly read.

Now, regarding the next possibility—comprehension is good but reading speed is compromised—let's pause and think about this. How will comprehension be improved if reading speed isn't improved? Isn't efficient reading a prerequisite to enhancing comprehension? To put it another way, what's the point of learning to read faster if you're able to comprehend what you're reading anyway?

When your comprehension is good, but you don't read well, it's because your mind relies on the mental cues it's getting about the passage. Your mind isn't relying on the words written on the page; rather, it's assuming that certain words *will* be written on the page and operates from that mindset. However, this strategy can give you the wrong idea about the subject because you're making assumptions and not actually reading.

To tackle this habit, you need to understand the

problem entirely and continue to practice reading at a slow pace so you don't skip certain terms or assume what the words are. Consider using a pointer to guide you so you can read line by line in a sophisticated manner.

The 4-Stage Strategy for Speed Reading

Allow me to introduce you to the four stages we'll be exploring in the upcoming chapters. Using this strategy will help you gain a deeper understanding of the techniques used in this process and familiarize you with the sequence.

1.   TRAINING

Training is critical to creating a firm foundation on this journey. Training refers to developing dedication and having the genuine will to learn. Additionally, this chapter involves training your eyes and discovering your secret weapon, which will be an effective tool. We will focus on training in Chapter 3.

2. PRE-READING

This stage involves getting a general idea of the text along with maintaining a comfortable posture, ensuring the best place to speed read, and eliminating noise from your surroundings. Further, the pre-reading component introduces the four essential P's of pre-reading: previewing, predicting, prior knowledge, and purpose. Once you go through these steps and evaluate your needs, you'll have an enhanced understanding of your purpose, which will help you to achieve the desired outcome. Also, we'll go through setting your reading goals and getting into the zone for speed reading so you're free from external distractions and keenly focused on what you're doing. We will discuss Pre-reading in Chapter 4.

3. SPEED READING

This stage focuses on the seven techniques involved in the process of speed reading. Guiding yourself with a pointer—i.e., a finger, pen, or card to keep your eyes traveling along one line while reading—can be a great help to keep you focused and proceeding smoothly. Skimming, scanning, word grouping, skipping, stopping your inner monologue, and, finally, eliminating regression—rereading the words—are additional steps in the speed-reading process. While skimming helps you to go through a page quickly, scanning does the opposite. Instead of previewing the whole page, scanning ensures that you locate particular pre-determined words on the page. Skipping involves ignoring certain content altogether, and word grouping is reading a group of words instead of reading individual ones. We will explore these techniques in chapter 5.

4.   COMPREHENSION   AND RETENTION

Chapter 6 will expand on the final stage, which focuses on comprehension and retaining the information you have read.

Chapter 3: Training

Be Dedicated

Dedication, in my opinion, is the only true measure of a person's commitment to his or her job or task. We see great examples of dedication around us: Elon Musk, Jeff Bezos, Jack Ma, and many others. If you happen to come across any of their interviews, you'll realize they didn't achieve success overnight. It took them years to build what they have today. Not only were they committed, but they were also patient and persistent.

Unfortunately, the virtues of dedication, commitment, and hard work are less appealing and respected in today's society. Most people seek instant results and "get-rich-quick" schemes that don't require investing large amounts of time and effort. They want everything now, be it success, gratification, or comfort. However, the truth is that anything undertaken without dedication and persistence tends to rise quickly but quickly falls as well. That's the law of true dedication.

Make sure you create realistic goals and then be dedicated to achieving them. If you want to be physically strong, you need to hit the gym 6 to 10 hours a week to gain your desired results in three months. But, think about it. How long will your body remain fit if you lose the dedication after those three months and stop going to the gym altogether? This is why you have to create meaningful, realistic goals that not only motivate you to work hard today but that you can maintain to become a better version of yourself tomorrow.

Set long-term goals, and evaluate them over time. Think in terms of months, years, and even decades, so you have the bigger picture in mind and a reasonably large frame of reference from which to evaluate your progress. Believe in yourself, acknowledge your strengths, and keep moving toward your long-term goals.

The process of speed reading uses these same principles. Visualize how many books you want to finish in the next two years. This will automatically give you an idea of how committed you are to learning and applying speed-reading techniques. Make realistic, practical, and measurable goals for yourself, and get going on learning how to speed read.

There are numerous activities in life that you may have always wanted to try. For instance, you might want to learn how to ski if you move to a country like Canada. You may want to try a sport you've never tried before. Indeed, you may be motivated to do this because you're in a new environment and around new people. You want to make the most of the situation, but ask yourself this: Am I dedicated? Are you genuinely committed to giving your best to the new adventure, or are you motivated just by wanting to keep up with your peers?

You need to ask yourself this same question with anything new that you want to adopt into your life. When considering learning speed reading, ask yourself this: Why do I want to acquire this skill? How will it benefit me? Am I willing to put the time, effort, and energy into this? Will I be dedicated enough to see this journey to the end?

One way to strengthen your willpower is to work on your goals every day, no matter how briefly. Sometimes your motivation will need a little nudge in the right direction. One great way to stay inspired is to think about the end result—how it will feel to have this amazing new skill. There may be many obstacles on your path to achieving your goals, but it's ultimately up to you to decide how dedicated and successful you'll be.

Train Your Eyes

As discussed earlier in this book, your eyes are vital in speed reading, so you need to ensure that you take care of them. Just like your back gets sore when you sit for too long, your eyes get dry and irritated when you use

54

them too intensely for too long. When you focus your eyes on a particular activity for too long, they may get itchy, tired, or unfocused.

Eyes use natural mechanisms to stay lubricated that include blinking to keep them moist. The natural fluid in the eyes keeps them lubricated, enabling you to open them when you wake up in the morning. It also keeps your eyes functioning healthily. However, when your eyes are focused on reading for hours, and you don't blink frequently, they may become dry, which may lead to irritation on the surface of the eye, fatigue of the eye muscles, and, commonly, headache.

Therefore, specialists strongly advise that you train your eyes to focus while preventing them from becoming tired. A suitable method is to allow your eyes to gaze at something in the distance every so often while you're reading to allow them to rest. Research shows that we can focus on any given subject for no more than 20 minutes at a time to retain good eye health. Knowing this, it may be beneficial to close your eyes for two to three minutes or allow them to gaze unfocused at something in the distance, and then start again.

Here are some practical exercises you can try. See what works best for you, and get started today.

- Thumb-to-Thumb Glancing

This exercise works to enhance the flexibility of your eyeball while strengthening your focus. It helps you increase your vision span by having a broader range of content in each fixation, enabling you to read faster.

Instructions

There's no hard-and-fast rule regarding whether you should be sitting or standing to do this exercise. All you have to do is keep your head motionless and extend both your arms out to the sides. Without moving your head, glance at your left thumb and then at the right. Do this three times. You can repeat this exercise three times a day to enhance your eye movement flexibility.

- Eye Writing

This exercise helps you increase the range of motion of your eyes, thereby maintaining their flexibility.

Instructions

This exercise involves writing with your eyes. Choose a wall that's far from you yet still clearly visible. On that wall, write your name or anyone else's. For instance, if I choose to write "Sophie," I start from one corner of the wall, begin with the letter 'S,' and make all the curves of the letters using my eyes as I write out the name.

- Hooded Eyes

This is the perfect exercise to indulge yourself when you need a little break from the screen or a book.

Instructions

Begin by closing your eyelids halfway. As you do this, you may instantly feel the urge to either close or open your eyes. However, refrain from doing either. Keep your eyes partially closed by looking at an object far away from you, and allow your gaze to soften and relax.

- Eyelid Squeeze

Squeezing your eyelids improves the blood flow to your facial region and the eyes in particular.

Instructions

To do this exercise, open your mouth and eyes as wide as possible as you inhale. You'll feel your mouth opening up beyond its standard limit and your jaws getting a stretch. As you exhale, close your mouth, and squeeze your eyelids shut as firmly as possible. This will help to bring blood to your eyes and refresh them.

Discover Your Secret Weapon – Your Hand

Has it ever happened that you're reading a sentence in a book and, very smoothly, without any effort, you move on to the following line only to realize you've skipped a line?

As an illustration, try reading this:

"The boy was whimpering because he was lost in the woods. His mother had asked him to stay with her, but when he saw a deer and wanted to pet it, he followed the hungry animal instead of his parent."

Now, let me show you what often happens when you don't have a pacer (a pen, a finger, a card), and your mind is distracted. This may be what you read:

"The boy was whimpering, saw a deer, and wanted to pet it; he followed the hungry animal instead of his parent."

You unintentionally moved to the following line and skipped the words on the same line as if it was all part of the flow. This is precisely what happens when you don't direct your eyes toward something specific in what you're reading.

One popular practice among speed readers is to use a visual pacer to keep them focused precisely on the words they just read and those coming after. When people become adept at this, they move their visual pacer so extraordinarily quickly that you're left wondering whether they're just skimming or actually getting a grasp on the content.

It's a scientific fact that the human eye is attracted to objects in motion. Whether it's an airplane flying above you, a sparrow hopping on a branch outside your window that you can see from the corner of your eye, or the activity of characters in a movie, your attention is drawn to that motion. It's the same phenomenon as an infant becoming fascinated when we shake a rattle in front of their eyes. Since they've recently emerged from their mother's womb, their visual span is yet to be developed and is stimulated whenever they see moving objects.

Therefore, it's essential to use your finger or another pacing device as a guide when increasing your reading speed. This will prevent you from skipping lines, your brain won't be distracted by other things, and your eyes will stay focused. Doing just this will increase your reading speed by 20%. If you don't wish to use your finger or a pen, you can use anything with a straight edge, such as a card or a ruler. This will help your eyes only focus on what's written directly above the straight edge of the card. Keep going until you reach the end of the page, and continue on the next page.

Using a visual pacer may not be as effective when you're reading on a computer screen. Of course, you wouldn't want to use your finger on the screen, and using the mouse to move from left to right may be tedious.

To tackle this situation while reading on any screen, you can use speed-reading software that's user-friendly, free, and available in abundance online. You'll have to paste in the content you want to read and set a timer for the duration you wish to read the particular content. Calculating the number of words in the document and considering your desired reading time, the software flashes the words in front of you so your eyes can easily track the flashed terms and not stray to the line beneath them.

Practice Stretching Your Reading Limit

For the moment, let's set comprehension to the side and think about how fast you'd be able to read if you weren't concerned about comprehension. If you're not required to understand the meaning of the content you're reading, your reading pace would be significantly higher.

In the beginning, to get the hang of reading at a faster pace, it's recommended that you begin to train your mind by setting a one-minute timer for a passage having approximately 400 to 500 words. If you're a beginner, your goal should be to get through the whole page. This training will help you become accustomed to the reading pace and, once you achieve that, you can gradually move to better comprehension and retention. Remember, this is just a training exercise; you're allowed to sacrifice comprehension and retention as you become comfortable with reading faster. You can keep track of your progress by setting a shorter amount of time with each passage you read. Go faster each time, and see how much you can comprehend.

Tackle Bad Habits

The first step to tackling and overcoming any issue hindering your reading speed is to be aware of it and accept it. Unwillingness to accept your flaws will make you even more resistant to new learning. Therefore, identify the bad reading habits you may have so you can begin to address them. Only after you know what needs to be changed will you be determined to work on it.

Vocalization

When we vocalize every word while reading, we simply can't read quickly. In addition, vocalizing while reading causes fatigue.

One-Word-at-a-Time Readers

It may seem odd, but there are people who read each word and stop to consider its meaning before moving on to the next word. This practice decreases their reading rate—i.e., word per minute (WPM)—and inhibits the ability to comprehend the sentence's meaning as a whole. In fact, the one-word-at-a-time reader will have to invest more time and energy attempting to grasp the meaning of each word and then taking in the meaning of the sentence as a whole.

Regression

Regression refers to slipping onto a primitive mode of development when faced with a stressful situation. With regard to reading, regression refers to moving to

63

the beginning of a sentence to reread it. We tend to reread sentences because we feel we didn't retain the meaning of what we just read, or we have a sense we were distracted while reading that sentence. With time, regression becomes more of a habit than a genuine need.

Distorted Expectations of Reading

As children, we may have been rewarded with 20 minutes of video games or given our favorite candy after finishing a storybook. However, this practice of providing a reward for reading creates a belief that there's nothing inherently enjoyable about reading—that it is, in fact, a chore—when the opposite is actually the case.

Focus – Get in the Zone

In July 2007, Anne Jones of England set a world record by reading the last book of the Harry Potter series in 47 minutes and 1 second. Sounds impossible, right? How on earth was she able to do it? Had you been in her place, you may have read only one chapter in 47 minutes or maybe just a few pages.

Starting to read a book can be challenging and requires effort and persistence until you get used to the book's theme and start enjoying the reading process. When you start a new book, you must familiarize yourself with the characters, the dialogue, the author's writing style, and, most importantly, the story itself. You may zone out at the start if you find the beginning of the book mundane and not compelling as you turn the pages. Didn't Anne Jones have these same challenges? Didn't she have trouble getting oriented to the style and story?

Speed reading isn't about reading fast all the time. It requires using our intelligence to determine when we should read at a faster pace, when we should slow down to more fully grasp the concept or story, and when we should skip words or phrases altogether. Knowing what to do in different situations depends on how accurately we've pre-read the subject. We'll explore pre-reading in the next chapter.

You won't be able to get in the zone of speed reading overnight. It's an inevitable truth that you'll have to keep practicing, not only when reading books but any other printed material—your email, an informative article, or even some headlines on the television. Getting in the zone means you should be able to adapt quickly to the particular reading situation and, for that, you need constant practice.

Try getting into the zone when you're in the waiting room at the dentist's office. Grab a magazine and start reading. Do it when you're out in the morning having a solo breakfast. Take out your phone, open up a news article, and start reading.

CHAPTER 4: PRE-READING

In this chapter, we'll be focusing on the critical strategies of pre-reading. We'll cover three simple steps that will not only boost your reading speed but your confidence as well.

Step 1: Prepare

Before starting to pre-read, you need to address the following:

Distractions

Distractions can seem impossible to avoid. However, studies have shown that distractions cause a massive loss of productivity. You need to create an optimum environment for reading. A peaceful and conducive reading environment can help you to concentrate better. To maintain that ambiance, remove as many distractions as possible. Silence electronic devices. Notifications, incoming calls, and texts are distractions. Make sure you turn your phone, tablet, and laptop off while reading to help you stay focused and increase your reading speed. Additionally, reduce all background noise. Choose a space where there isn't even a noisy fan revolving to disturb your thoughts.

Lighting

Choose a room where the lighting isn't too bright or too dim. Make sure the light is adequate, and you don't have to strain your eyes to easily read the letters on the page. Remember, your eyes are the most essential part of your body when it comes to reading. Therefore, you don't want to strain them. The best lighting for reading is diffused lighting or lighting that comes from several sources to prevent glare on the page.

Body Posture

Correct body posture is critical when you're reading, as well as to maintain your health and improve your concentration. Make sure your legs have proper support and aren't dangling from the chair. If your feet don't touch the floor, grab a stool to support your feet and legs and keep your posture stable.

The next consideration is to sit up straight in the chair with your back pressed firmly against it. More than half of the population slouches when sitting. It seems to be a natural tendency to slouch whenever we're sitting in a chair. If not addressed, this poor habit can lead to chronic neck pain and backache. Correcting your posture may be uncomfortable at first, but if you're committed to reaching your goal and maintaining good health, it will benefit you to make this a permanent habit.

Hold the book at a comfortable distance from your eyes, so you don't have to move your head forward to read. Hold the book close enough that you can easily read and your back remains straight. A book is best held at a 45-degree angle to your eyes.

Step 2: Set Your Reading Goal

We know how important it is to set goals for ourselves. Establishing reading goals before diving into a book sets the tone to achieve the results you expect from yourself. To improve your reading ability, it's essential to set rules for yourself—and, more important, abide by them. Set aside a specific time each day for reading. It can be 15 minutes or an hour, but try to read around the same time each day.

Determine your purpose for reading – Why are you reading this book?

- For pleasure and enjoyment
- To learn something new
- To acquire specific information
- To identify the central theme
- To develop a detailed and critical understanding

Additionally, ask yourself self-reflective questions, like, "What kind of a reader am I right now?" "How much do I want to be capable of reading?" "Why do I want to learn to read faster?" These are fundamental questions that will serve as the basis for your motivation and will keep you moving forward.

Step 3: Pre-Reading

The four P's of pre-reading are previewing, predicting, prior knowledge, and purpose.

Previewing

Previewing means reading to understand a subject as a whole instead of as a collection of words or sentences. This is a rapid kind of reading that allows you to get a general sense of what a passage, article, or book is about and how it's organized.

In previewing an article or passage, you look at the first paragraph, the initial sentence of each section, and the last sentence of each section. Some of the questions you should be asking yourself during this process are:

What is this section about?
What's the title of the section?
What's the nature of the writing? Is it a description, an explanation, an argument, a narrative (history)?
Is the text divided into parts? How is it organized?

71

Are there any illustrations, numbers, italicized words, or names in the text?

Predicting

The next 'P' of pre-reading occurs after you preview the text. You predict what you're likely to achieve from the content.

Prior Knowledge

This is the phase where you ask yourself whether you have any prior knowledge or insight about the topic you're reading about. You may ask yourself questions like:

What do I already know about this topic?
Have I read about this subject before?
If yes, what do I recall about it?

Purpose

This process involves evaluating the author's purpose to develop an accurate idea of what they want to convey to their audience, what motivated them to write on this particular subject, and what they expect from their readers.

CHAPTER 5: SPEED READING

Step 4: Choose Your Visual Pacer

As stated earlier, a visual pacer can be a pen, finger, card, or ruler.

Here are a few benefits of using a visual pacer:
- It gives your eyes a limited area of words on which to stay focused.
- It enables your brain to stay alert and your eyes to move quicker.
- It tricks your brain into its highest level of concentration, and this helps prevent distraction.

73

- Your pacer stimulates movement, which alerts your brain to follow the line of words that it's being directed to.
- Most importantly, it helps you become a pro at speed reading.

Here are some of the pacing methods you can benefit from:

Single-Finger Methods

For beginners, getting used to the pacing strategy using only one finger is an excellent idea. It will keep you in your comfort zone while also helping you to explore a new way of tracking words.

1. Long, smooth underline **(Recommended)**: Begin by placing your index finger at the beginning of each line just under the words you're reading. As your finger moves along, read above it. When your finger comes to the end of the line, quickly bring it back to the beginning of the following line and begin the process again.

2. Left-pointer pull: To use this method, curl all the fingers of your hand toward your palm

except your index finger, and place it on the left side of the line. Remember that you don't have to move your finger across the whole line; instead, quickly move your forefinger down to the left side of the following line when your eyes complete the line above and meet your forefinger on the next line below.

3. Right-pointer pull: As the name suggests, this technique is the opposite of the left-pointer bull. Instead of putting your forefinger on the left side of the line, you place it on the right side. Also, instead of reading from the pointer, now you read from the beginning of the sentence to the pointer. Keep moving your right pointer in a downward motion as your eyes finish each line and meet it at the end before beginning the new line.

4. Center-pointer pull: This is yet another technique for beginners that helps guide the eyes. Using this technique, the index finger isn't placed on the right side or the left side; instead, the finger is placed in the middle of the first line and travels downward from that spot

to stabilize eye motion and concentration as you read.

Step 5: Skimming

Skimming is used to quickly identify the main ideas of a text and is done at speed three to four times faster than regular reading.

The purpose of deliberate skimming is to get a rough idea about the topic being discussed. In deliberate skimming, you follow the guidelines below to grasp the overall meaning of the words in a well-organized manner.

Conversely, haphazard skimming involves irregular movement of the eyes and guarantees no comprehension during the process. It's like reading random words in a paragraph without paying attention to the topic sentence or the concluding sentence.

How to Skim:
- Read the title.
- Read the introduction or the first paragraph.

- Read the first sentence of every other paragraph.
- Read any headings and subheadings.
- Notice any pictures, charts, or graphs.
- Notice any italicized or boldfaced words or phrases.
- Read the summary or last paragraph.

You might use skimming to:

- Get an overview of the news in a newspaper or on a website.
- Browse through a book to determine if you want to read it.
- Look through the television guide to see what's on one evening.
- Flick through a catalog to see what's on offer.
- Look through the options in a Google search to see what results seem most relevant to what you're looking for.

EXERCISE

Skim the paragraph below and try to answer the questions that follow it:

"Here's something to think about the next time you go shopping. Have you ever noticed how many **shopping carts** are available when you go to the supermarket? In my experience, it *seems like hundreds*! But how about the number of hand baskets? Invariably *I struggle to find even one*, especially when I only need a few items. Why might this be the case? Well, it seems to be **a tactic used to encourage us to buy more**. If you're walking around with an empty shopping cart, you're more tempted to fill it, so if you're planning on only doing a quick shop, always try to find a basket. It will be lighter, easier to use, and is sure to **save you money!**"

Now, test your skimming skills by answering these questions:

1. What can you find in large numbers at a supermarket?

2. Why might this be a problem?

3. How can you avoid spending more than you planned?

4. Why is it a good idea to use a handbasket instead of a shopping cart?

Step 6: Scanning

While skimming is about getting a general idea of a paragraph, scanning is more about finding a specific word or group of words. For instance, you scan the grocery bill if you are unsure about the price of broccoli. You search for particular amounts of revenue when you read a company's annual report. When filling out a deposit slip at the bank, you may scan for the place you have to sign.

Scanning is usually done after skimming, as the process of skimming helps you evaluate whether a given paragraph contains what you're looking for. Once the general idea of a topic is obtained and you've studied the organizational structure of the section, you can determine whether to scan for particular details.

The best way to scan is by selecting a keyword and then putting all your effort into searching for that word. For instance, if you want to obtain an answer to a specific question, you should pick a keyword from the question itself. For example, if you're studying an article on cancer statistics in the US, and you're looking for the mortality rate per year, make 'death rate' or 'mortality' your keyword and start looking for it. Once you find the particular word or phrase, reading the words in that sentence will allow you to find the answer to your question in an organized and efficient manner.

EXERCISE

Scan the following paragraph with these questions in mind:

1. The merchant was offered to sell his rice to which countries?
2. Why did the merchant refuse to sell his stock?
3. How were the merchant's plans ruined?

"There's a story is of a rich merchant who had the uncontrollable desire to rise higher than all others in the rice business. People called him successful because his rice inventories doubled in a few years, and the profits from his sales rose tremendously. One year, there was a bumper (full and large) rice crop in the country and, even after exports, lots of rice remained. The merchant recognized that this was a big opportunity, and he bought plenty of rice at cheap rates and stored it. He was hoping to earn fabulous profits in the coming years by selling his stores when rice was in short supply. It so happened that the government approached the merchant with an offer to sell his rice inventory to Saudi Arabia and Kuwait at quite high rates. He would realize a profit of millions of dollars in just a few days. However, he refused to supply rice for export, stating that he'd earn a few billion if he sold the rice domestically later on. God or luck willed otherwise. There were heavy rains soon after, and the nearby river was in high flood and overflowed its banks. All the inventories of the rich merchant were flooded. His stored rice was spoiled, and all his plans were ruined. This demonstrates how his planning and action proved the truth of the saying that it never pays to overreach oneself."

Step 7: Word Grouping or Chunking

When was the last time you read individual words just for the purpose of noting every single word? For most of us, the answer is, "In elementary school." At that time, we were young and at our most primitive stage of learning. We were taught to spell out words when we began reading a complete sentence. However, as we grow into adults, we must get over that habit and start

81

reading in a way that makes it possible to more quickly and easily comprehend the meaning of the sentences. That's where chunking comes into play.

Chunking is a famous strategy used by many to read at a faster rate. It involves combining two to three words in our visual field so we read them simultaneously. Chunking is a proven strategy to stimulate visualization of any piece of text or group of numbers. Combining two or three words gives us more data to imagine the context more completely. For instance, if I say the word 'apple' out of the blue, you may be able to visualize the fruit in your imagination, but there's no other information to contextualize this word. You'll be able to imagine the fruit, but you'll be incapable of making any sense out of it. What about that apple?

Now, instead of just saying one word, if I say, "Please eat an apple," does that give you a fuller picture? Are you automatically able to comprehend what I'm trying to say? Is the context transparent now? Yes. This is what happens when we group words together. It allows us to read faster and increases our comprehension level by enabling us to visualize a scenario.

When it comes to clumping, it's recommended that we take baby steps. Start with grouping two words only and use your index finger to guide you to the next chunk of words. This is the beginner level. Once you feel the beginner level is too easy and you can comprehend these smaller chunks easily, you can move on to the intermediate level. In this level, group three to four words in a sentence together and read them in one glance. You'll eventually move to the highest level, in which you chunk five words together.

Step 8: Skipping

Skipping, also known as selective reading, refers to intentionally skipping portions of the written content because they're irrelevant to your needs. An advanced and experienced reader can quickly recognize what can be ignored while reading any content.

In today's world, almost everything relies on reading, so that means you have a lot on your reading plate practically every day—whether that be websites, articles, magazines, pamphlets, or books. The skill of skipping will help you look for important and specific details and ignore the text that won't benefit you. You can skip a paragraph if you realize it contains mundane details or covers nothing you need to know.

Step 9: Reduce Subvocalization

Subvocalization is a common habit among many readers. It refers to saying words in your head while reading, and it's one of the primary reasons people read slowly and have trouble improving their reading speed.

Reducing subvocalization focuses on minimizing your inner monologue by having a peaceful state of mind and achieving inner tranquility. When reading, the words in front of us swirl in our mind and may confuse us, eventually creating an experience of what we call a "surreal read." If this inner monologue doesn't stop, you're constantly bothered while reading because you hear the words in your mind, which interferes with your ability to easily read what's before you.

When you began reading in your early years, you were taught to read out loud. Once you could read well enough, you were probably told to start saying the words in your head rather than aloud. This is how the

84

habit of subvocalization usually originates. Many people continue reading this way for the rest of their life. You don't need to say every word in your head to understand what you're reading and, if you want to start reading faster, you need to stop this bad habit.

Subvocalization can occur in three stages:
- Stage 1 – Moving your lips as you read but without emitting a sound
- Stage 2 – No longer moving your lips during reading, but your vocal cords vibrate as if you're speaking
- Stage 3 – Mouthing the words to yourself silently

Here are a few ways to minimize subvocalization:
- Use a visual pacer.
- Listen to music while you read. Be aware that you need to choose a piece of serene and calming music and not music with a loud beat, as your brain will be further distracted by that. For most people, classical music has been shown to improve concentration, maximize reading speed, and reduce subvocalization.

- Concentrate, so you're able to focus on the words in what you're reading, but distract yourself skillfully, so you don't vocalize them. For example, try chewing a piece of bubble gum when reading. While your mouth is engaged in chewing, your brain will be invested in reading and comprehending the written material.

Step 10: Eliminate Regression

Regression is the unnecessary rereading of material. Reading something twice can result in a huge waste of time. When you reread sentences, you lose the flow and structure of the text, and your overall understanding of the topic decreases. This reading practice most often originates during childhood, and some of us haven't been able to break the bad habit. This habit often becomes more of an obsession than an attempt to ensure better comprehension.

Regression is more likely to happen when we aren't genuinely immersed in the reading or are reading something we're not motivated to read because someone told us to. When that happens, your brain quickly finds an escape, and you lose your focus in the book.

Be mindful of regression, and don't allow yourself to reread material unless you absolutely have to. The best practice for eliminating regression is to use a visual pacer. This helps to develop coordination of your eye movement with your hand movement and enhances your ability to stay focused on what you're reading.

CHAPTER 6 - COMPREHENSION AND RETENTION

After thoroughly practicing each speed-reading technique, identifying which one works best for you, and learning to read faster, what's most important is how well you comprehend and retain the information.

Active reading is the process used to maximize comprehension capability. It also focuses on strategies that enable you to recall what you've read quickly and efficiently.

Active Reading

If you want to practice actively reading a paragraph or section in a book, for instance, first grab a piece of paper and a pen. After you've gotten an overview of what the section is about by skimming it, ask yourself what's driving you to read this text and comprehend it fully. Only if you have a compelling answer to this question will you understand the subject thoroughly. Ask yourself how it will benefit you to read this paragraph actively and how doing so will help you in the future. Will it help you land a job or increase your knowledge of a particular subject? Answering such questions will provide clarity and purpose to what you're doing.

Once you've answered these questions, start reading, and underline, highlight, or place an asterisk to mark the most important sentences in the paragraph. Look for any terminology, descriptions, or vocabulary that you're unfamiliar with, and take the time to go through the dictionary and become familiar with these words.

Pay close attention to the topic sentence, which usually appears in the first paragraph of an article or chapter,

90

to help you grasp the main idea of the content. It's always in the first paragraph that the author states what he'll be discussing in that section or article. Though it isn't plainly apparent like a table of contents at the beginning of a book, the topic sentence provides guidance on what you're about to read.

It will help when you're doing active reading to have the goal of gaining in-depth knowledge of the topic. It's mandatory not only to read the lines and move forward smoothly but also to test yourself along the way and write down any questions you have. Once you've finished reading, use your browser, a book, or maybe your teacher to help walk you through any confusion and find clarity about the topic.

Try to visualize and create mental examples of the statements you're reading. You can also make notes, charts, or graphs to ensure that you understood what you read, and this will make it easier for you to read through the material the next time. For instance, if you've just read Newton's third law of motion, try to think of practical and relatable examples. When have you witnessed the third law of motion with your own eyes? Perhaps it was when you were bouncing a tennis ball on the ground while playing with your mates. The ball would have lifted itself off the ground with an equal and opposite force to that by which you threw it toward the ground. This exercise of thinking of real-life examples may take a while to learn, but it will give you clarity like no other technique.

After reading an entire essay or chapter, you should be able to rewrite it in your own words. This will ensure that you can teach the topic or a particular concept to someone else, if need be. Research shows that teaching is one of the most effective ways to evaluate your learning.

The main difference between passive and active reading is that you have no control or authority over your pace when you read passively. In passive reading, you read at the same speed, regardless of the relevance of the topic. You don't preview the essay, article, or chapter before reading it to get a general idea of what the text is about; instead, you dive straight into reading. When passively reading, you don't prepare questions after you complete your reading, and no thorough evaluation takes place of the information you just received.

Contrary to this, active reading enables the reader to actively engage in the written content and relate to it. It increases their comprehension level while allowing them to visualize the knowledge in bits and pieces and then bring them together to form a cohesive concept.

Retention

Retention is the process of transporting information learned from your short-term memory into your long-term memory for recall in the future. However, it's not as easy as it sounds.

A study conducted to measure retention in an organization of 1,000 employees inferred that each employee wasted about 10,000 hours per year trying to memorize things that were spoken about during training sessions. Not only that, the research further suggested that when these employees weren't able to recall the desired information, they wasted an additional 5,800 hours trying to look up that data in their notes. This gives you some idea of how

93

exhausting and time-consuming searching for lost information can be.

It's almost futile to learn new things if you can't store that knowledge in your brain for an extended period of time and be able to retrieve it. With this in mind, strategies have been devised to boost the capacity to recall previously learned information with minimal effort.

Here are a few of those strategies to help you along your journey:

TELL A STORY

Telling a story when we learn something new has been proven to improve retention by 22%. You can easily do this by constructing a story in your mind that includes all the facts you just learned in what you read. If you think about it, the same principle is being applied here as with seeing words as a whole rather than as individual words. Telling a story, to yourself or another person, that summarizes what you've read allows you to integrate what you learned effectively. This substantially enhances the chances that it will be stored in your subconscious and retrievable with little effort.

ONE-WORD RETENTION

This technique focuses on eliminating the superficial and reducing the content to just one word. This one word becomes a trigger for all the information associated with it. Condensing the content and meaning of a whole paragraph, for instance, into one word should be done wisely to ensure proper retention.

Let's suppose you've just read a short story about two best friends spending their entire childhood together only to betray each other on Christmas Eve, ending their friendship forever. Now, the one word you can choose to summarize this short story effectively is 'betrayal.' Once you recall this word, the whole story of the two friends will come flooding back to you.

WRITE DOWN YOUR THOUGHTS

Writing down your opinions about a story, novel, or book helps you retrieve the whole story, primarily because your thoughts are associated with your opinions. To elaborate, you form a perception of what you've read, label it as "good" or "bad," and that perception is stored in your brain. When you later reflect on that opinion, it brings to mind what you read that caused you to form that perspective.

CONCLUSION

Indeed, you've come a long way now that you've reached the end of this book. We began this journey with a promise, as you might remember. I promised that, by the end of this book, you'd be reading faster than when you began it. Not only that, I promised to keep you interested and focused while reading this book, as this text will serve as the cornerstone of your new journey. That commitment ends here because your comprehension level is better, and you're ready to dive into dozens of books.

It's inevitable in today's world that you can't avoid reading. From interpreting a signboard to comprehending the terminology of a Ph.D. dissertation, you need to master the essential skill of reading. To maximize your command of the content you come across, speed reading is tremendously valuable.

Numerous studies have been conducted in the last decade on this process, and the consensus is that speed reading can have a profound impact on an individual's life. Broadening vision span, improving environmental conditions for reading, and accelerating reading speed bring about positive changes in an individual's cognitive functioning and, of course, social relationships.

Now that you've completed this book, I'm confident you've discovered new possibilities and potential within you. You have a broader sense of what you can achieve, and having this sense of confidence is an achievement in itself. You've learned how to evaluate what to read and also with what mindset to read it with. Moving forward, you're motivated and aware of the multitude of benefits speed reading can provide and the opportunities it offers.

I want all my readers to know and believe that their mind is in their control. Often, our brain is overwhelmed by our emotions and negative thoughts, which may eventually start to control us instead of us controlling them. Only you have the power to change what you think and think what you want. Gain control over your mind and start believing in the possibility that you can achieve what you train your mind to believe in. Know in your heart that the ability to speed read is in your own hands. If you make a conscious effort, invest time and dedication—not to mention regular practice—you'll get the hang of it. One day, speed reading will seem like it's always been a natural activity for you. You won't have to focus on your concentration; it will emerge naturally, without thinking about it, just like the beating of your heart.

Knowing the benefit of these valuable techniques, you can regularly check in with yourself to evaluate how your reading and comprehension have improved. Reading this book alone won't assure that you'll be able to speed read for the rest of your life. You need to maintain consistency, regular practice, and genuine dedication to keep your reading chops honed.

In addition, you can get help from speed-reading software and apps that provide a designated pathway to follow so you don't get lost along the way. Using such apps will also help you maintain a healthy routine of practice and reading books, as these many of these technologies incorporate reminders and alerts.

Writing this book for my fellow readers has given me a real sense of satisfaction. Not only has it shown me what wonders I can do with my writing, but it's also made me aware of what I have yet to do.

One more thing

If you enjoyed this book and found it helpful, I'd be very grateful if you'd post a short review on Amazon. Your support makes a difference, and I read all the reviews personally to get your feedback and make this book even better. I love hearing from my readers, and I'd really appreciate it if you leave your honest feedback.

Thank you for reading!

BONUS CHAPTER

I would like to share a sneak peek into another one of my books that I think you will enjoy. The book is titled ***"How to be Charismatic, Develop Confidence, and Exude Leadership: The Miracle Formula for Magnetic Charisma, Defeating Anxiety, and Winning at Communication"***

This book will show you how to become a charismatic leader, develop sharp social skills, and become a passionate extrovert so that you can skyrocket your career, have healthier relationships, and grow genuine confidence and self-esteem!

But what if you're shy, introverted, and insecure? What if you feel like you don't have what it takes to grow and conquer your deepest dreams and desires? Don't worry! The simple tools you can learn right now are only a few clicks away!

The tips, tricks, and exercises given in this book will make you more attractive to anyone who meets you,

103

including friends, coworkers, bosses, and romantic interests! This book will teach you how to:

- Discover and grow genuine charisma and magnetic appeal by tapping into your inner goodness, beauty, and passion to motivate yourself and others
- Start developing social skills to make new acquaintances, spread your influence, and increase personal power
- Nurture deep, meaningful, healthy, and mutually supportive relationships
- Build true, unshakeable confidence by nurturing your authenticity and self-esteem
- Become an effective listener to establish deep connections and detect people's needs, desires, and motives
- Convey and read body language to exude confidence, positivity, and strength
- Click with people around you to compel them with your magnetic charisma
- Increase your popularity and extend your social network

- Grow a leader's confidence and mindset by setting goals, contributing to the group, and motivating and supporting others
- Leave a positive, memorable first impression by making others feel comfortable, heard, and important
- Develop leadership communication skills, such as listening, interacting with individuals and groups, telling stories, and resolving conflicts
- Develop presence and magnetism to attract people all around, spread your message with passion and clarity, and grow talent to persuade people into doing what you want
- Practice an assertive attitude so that you can stop being shy, learn to say no, stand up for yourself without being aggressive, and set healthy boundaries that honor you and the people around you

Hop on a train toward the discovery of your hidden charisma, strengths, and potentials. This book shows you how to leverage simple, affordable, and accessible resources like knowledge and your own inborn talents to find your authentic self and showcase it to the world. No more hiding! The world deserves to see you! Start your journey right now and notice how you're becoming more socially competent and confident on the very same day!

Enjoy this free chapter!

Do you want to become the best version of yourself? Do you want to become memorable, appeal to people, and find personal and business success? Do you want to overcome shyness and insecurity and become more authentic and popular?

If you want all these things, it means that you have everything it takes to become a charismatic leader, and this book will show you exactly how to do that! *How to be Charismatic, Develop Confidence, and Exude Leadership: The Miracle Formula for Magnetic Charisma, Defeating Anxiety, and Winning at Communication* will help you get from where you are now to where you want to be by developing ten crucial leadership skills!

This book is for everyone looking to develop social skills, establish deep relationships, open themselves up to the world, and attract people with their bulletproof confidence and intoxicating charisma. Don't believe this can be you? Just wait!

This book will show you the exact techniques and give you the right tools to find the deeply hidden seed of charisma and grow it until it bursts and shines through you in a blinding, jaw-dropping aura that attracts people like moths are drawn to a flame.

How will this book do this for you? It's quite simple. This book will teach you all about charisma and magnetic appeal that you can start nurturing and growing today on any budget just by reaching deep down into the most beautiful depths of your inner being. This book will show you how to find and grab your positive values, strengths, and talents and make them your trademark.

Upon learning how to harvest the fruits of charisma, you'll learn how to develop social skills needed to extend your network of acquaintances, enrich your relationships, upscale your career, and influence people to get what you want. This book will show you how to become an active, engaged, and empathetic listener who makes a killer first impression and leaves people hungry for your presence.

To do this, you will find out how to get people to like you, and it will not be by putting on a mask. No! You will learn how to showcase your authentic self with the way you dress, speak, and shake hands so that everyone who meets you gets to know and love what they see. If you follow the instructions given in this book, you'll be able to show others the genuine, strong, and confident you. You will know how to appeal to people's hidden motivations and desires and connect with what you have in common.

Once you learn how to get people to like you, this book will show you how to form better and deeper relationships. You'll learn how to master the art of small talk to set the basis for deeper relationships and leverage these connections to give and take for the sake of mutual progress.

That's right! This book will show you how to become an altruistic, inspiring, and charismatic leader who wears their life's true purpose like one wears a suit and helps other people achieve their goals.

In this book, you will also find out how to become more assertive so that you can balance your feelings and attitude for more productive work and personal relationships. Aren't you tired of being shy and hiding in your cocoon? No more saying yes to things you don't want and doing things that step on your dignity and self-esteem just to please people! In this book, you will learn how to set healthy boundaries so that you can show people what they can and cannot do and what you are and aren't willing to tolerate. More importantly, you'll learn how to do this in a calm, respectful way—that is, respectful both to you and the people around you.

That's right! Assertiveness skills explained in this book will show you how to stand up for yourself without hostility and conflict. Isn't that amazing?

But how do you get there? How do you appeal to people to that extent if you're introverted and shy? What do you do if merely talking to people frightens you? Don't worry—you're covered!

This book will give you the basic knowledge for growing and nurturing true confidence and self-esteem based on your authentic personality and best traits. In this book, you'll learn how true confidence looks and how to start practicing it so that you know and understand that you're an infinitely worthy person who can rely on their talents and skills to advance in life. You will learn simple everyday techniques and tips to apply to feel better about yourself and truly believe in your own worth. But that's not all!

This book will tear the misconception that loving yourself means being selfish, and it will show you how to be respectful, truthful, and empathetic. Aside from learning how to become a leader, you will learn how to become a leader who gives and contributes to their group or organization. You will learn how to share ideas and feedback that build everyone up so that you and the people around you are successfully working toward a common goal.

This book will also show you how to use the best of your abilities to observe and read people, as well as use your appearance, performance, and body language to speak and spread your authentic message. Following the principles and instructions given in this book will help you trade the best of your strengths for respect and popularity with your friends, coworkers, and family. Simply put, this book will show you how to reach into the best you have and share it with the world, and then you will receive the sweet fruits of your charismatic labor.

Don't wait another minute! Your hidden potentials, core values, and infinite strengths are waiting to be discovered, grown, and plucked to bring you love, acceptance, and success you so deeply desire. With each minute that passes, your potentials are being wasted on self-defeating thoughts and self-sabotaging behaviors, and you are losing time and money on doing things for other people just because you're unable to say no!

Hurry up and start learning to make a great first impression. At the beginning of this book, you'll find out what you can do today so that people remember you and want to connect with you. Aren't you excited to lead?

What if I told you that how you come across during the first 30 seconds of meeting new people affects nearly 85 percent of your business success? What if I told you that the person you like takes only a split second to decide whether they like you or not. Doesn't it sound scary? That's because it is! Just imagine. Out of thousands of hours spent learning and doing hard work to build your career, mornings and evenings spent working out to get yourself in shape, all the planning that goes into your career, or all the charity work you do to make the world a better place, those initial 30 seconds determine the majority of your success!

If you still haven't freaked out, just wait. Remember the last time you made a new acquaintance. Maybe it was a bank clerk, a possible network connection, or your friend's friend who works for a major brand. It could even be your neighbor's coworker, who has a gorgeous son or daughter right about your age. What did these encounters look like? What did you say? How did you look? Were you clean and polished, or were you dressed in rags because you were cleaning your backyard?

How you carry yourself and act around other people determines your success regardless of your true skills, talents, and positive traits. Nailing that first impression can open many doors, point out shortcuts, and help you make long-term connections. But how do you do that? How do you make people remember you and want to talk to you in less than a minute? Lucky for you, you've come to the right place to get your answer.

Right before we get into the strategies for making an awesome first impression, let's briefly address why this is a challenge in the first place. When you're about to meet someone new, your fight-or-flight response gets triggered. Your unconscious brain evaluates whether or not you feel safe around the particular person, and it is particularly keen on detecting anything that's potentially threatening. If you look into the dynamic of first encounters, the truth is that it includes two or more people who instantly start deciding whether the new person seems safe to be around or they're to be avoided. Now, the way this works is that your unconscious mind detects the general appearance, body language, and other peculiarities regarding the other person and makes conclusions based on that. The same goes for those who evaluate you. The best way to make a great first impression is to send out more "green flags" than "red flags." This means to dress and behave in ways that help people feel safe and eliminate those behaviors that, unconsciously, signal danger.

Having a positive attitude means allowing the best of you to shine through your attitude and conversations. However, this positivity needs to be genuine and not imposed (i.e., toxic positivity). It's important to remember to consistently work on how you see the world so that you're able to maintain a positive, optimistic outlook on a situation while acknowledging the present reality. A general rule might be that people prefer positive people. However, if your job is to market yourself as a grief consultant, to say that you should act punchy and upbeat would be wrong. In this situation, you should level your mindset to be empathetic with the people you talk to, but be positive-oriented in the way you send your messages and talk to them. When talking to people in a business setting or at a party, it would be appropriate to show your most confident, upbeat self. What do you do when that's inappropriate? Then you adjust to how you can make the situation better.

Toxic positivity, on the other hand, is present in people we perceive as disingenuous. These people make false claims and statements of not only their success but also what others can do. Their intentions are self-involved, and that's easy to notice. They can only fool those who are emotionally and mentally vulnerable—and even that is only temporary. So when speaking about positivity, keep in mind that I'm referring to a genuinely helpful, optimistic attitude in your appearance and mannerisms aimed at making everyone around you feel a bit better than they felt before they met you. At times, you will do this using jokes, and other times, it will be through consolation and the words of support.

Get your full copy today! ***"How to be Charismatic, Develop Confidence, and Exude Leadership: The Miracle Formula for Magnetic Charisma, Defeating Anxiety, and Winning at Communication"***

BOOKS BY RICHARD BANKS

How to be Charismatic, Develop Confidence, and
Exude Leadership: The Miracle Formula for Magnetic
Charisma, Defeating Anxiety, and Winning at
Communication

How to Stop Being Negative, Angry, and Mean:
Master Your Mind and Take Control of Your Life

How to Deal with Grief, Loss, and Death: A Survivor's
Guide to Coping with Pain and Trauma, and Learning
to Live Again

How to Deal With Stress, Depression, and Anxiety: A
Vital Guide on How to Deal with Nerves and Coping
with Stress, Pain, OCD and Trauma

The Positive Guide to Anger Management: The Most
Practical Guide on How to Be Calmer, Learn to Defeat
Anger, Deal with Angry People, and Living a Life of

Mental Wellness and Positivity

Develop a Positive Mindset and Attract the Life of Your Dreams: Unleash Positive Thinking to Achieve Unbound Happiness, Health, and Success

The Keys to Being Brilliantly Confident and More Assertive: A Vital Guide to Enhancing Your Communication Skills, Getting Rid of Anxiety, and Building Assertiveness

Personal Development Mastery 2 Books in 1: The Keys to being Brilliantly Confident and More Assertive + How to be Charismatic, Develop Confidence, and Exude Leadership

Positive Mindset Mastery 2 Books in 1: Develop a Positive Mindset and Attract the Life of Your Dreams + How to Stop Being Negative, Angry, and Mean

REFERENCES

(2021, 8 7). Retrieved from brainly.com: https://brainly.ph/question/6722178

5 Reasons Why Speed Reading Is Good For Your Brain. (2021, 8 1). Retrieved from https://irisreading.com/5-reasons-why-speed-reading-is-good-for-your-brain/: https://irisreading.com/5-reasons-why-speed-reading-is-good-for-your-brain/

Ashley Robinson. (2021, 8 4). *Does Speed Reading Work?* Retrieved from blog.prepscholar.com: https://blog.prepscholar.com/speed-reading-how-to#:~:text=Con%3A%20It's%20Exhausting!,them%20on%20a%20regular%20basis.

Bessie Cherry. (2021, 8 22). *5 Strategies to Promote Retention of Information*. Retrieved from https://truscribe.com/retention-of-information/: https://truscribe.com/retention-of-information/

brainly.co. (2021, 8 9). Retrieved from https://brainly.co.id/tugas/25231504: https://brainly.co.id/tugas/25231504

Eye Exercises for Speed Reading. (2021, 8 5). Retrieved from dummies.com:

https://www.dummies.com/education/langua
ge-arts/speed-reading/eye-exercises-for-
speed-reading/

Health Status Team. (2021, 8 1). *Reasons why some
people read slowly*. Retrieved from Health
Status Team:
https://www.healthstatus.com/health_blog/a
dd-adhd-attention-deficit/reasons-why-some-
people-read-slowly/

How Learning to Read Rewrites the Brain. (2021, 8
5). Retrieved from livescience.com:
https://www.livescience.com/59335-adults-
who-learn-to-read-show-profound-brain-
plasticity.html

How To Reduce Subvocalization. (2021, 8 7).
Retrieved from irisreading.com:
https://irisreading.com/how-to-reduce-
subvocalization/

It never pays to overreach oneself. (2021, 8 7).
Retrieved from
http://educationsight.blogspot.com/:
http://educationsight.blogspot.com/2014/04
/short-story-on-It-never-pays-to-overreach-
oneself.html

Joy, R. (2021, 8 1). Retrieved from
https://www.healthline.com/health/benefits-
of-reading-books

Lymph Cells and Tissues. (2021, 8 5). Retrieved from
lumen learning.comq:

https://courses.lumenlearning.com/boundles
s-ap/chapter/lymph-cells-and-tissues/

Lymph Node. (2021, 8 8). Retrieved from glosbe.com:
https://glosbe.com/en/hr/lymph%20node

Lymph Node. (2021, 8 8). Retrieved from glosbe.com:
https://glosbe.com/en/hr/lymph%20node

Lymph Nodes. (2021, 8 7). Retrieved from
med.libretexts.org:
https://med.libretexts.org/Bookshelves/Anat
omy_and_Physiology/Book%3A_Anatomy_a
nd_Physiology_(Boundless)/19%3A_Lympha
tic_System/19.3%3A_Lymph_Cells_and_Tiss
ues/19.3C%3A_Lymph_Nodes

Mark. (2021, 8 8). *8 Speed Reading Techniques To
Read Faster.* Retrieved from
courselounge.com:
https://www.courselounge.com/speed-
reading-techniques/

Proper Reading Posture for Speed Reading. (2021, 8
6). Retrieved from irisreading.com:
https://irisreading.com/proper-reading-
posture-for-speed-reading/

Richard Sutz, P. W. (2021, 8 1). *Debunking Speed-
Reading Myths.* Retrieved from
https://www.dummies.com/education/langua
ge-arts/speed-reading/debunking-speed-
reading-myths/

Skimming and Scanning. (2021, 8 7). Retrieved from
Skillswise:

http://teach.files.bbci.co.uk/skillswise/en05s kim-e3-f-skimming-and-scanning.pdf

Speed Reading. (2021, 8 1). Retrieved from mindtools.org: https://www.mindtools.com/speedrd.html

Summarize Written Text. (2021, 8 7). Retrieved from /thelearningbit.com: https://thelearningbit.com/100-ple-questions/

The Complete Idiot's Guide to Speed Reading (2008). (2021, 8 7). Retrieved from schoolbag.info: https://schoolbag.info/literature/speed/9.html

Tricks, Tips, and the Benefits of Pre-Reading Text. (2021, 8 5). Retrieved from thoughtco.com: https://www.thoughtco.com/prereading-definition-1691529

Yong Kang Chan. (2021, 8 1). *Personal Development.* Retrieved from lifehack.org: https://www.lifehack.org/articles/productivity/15-ways-help-you-read-more.html

Printed in Great Britain
by Amazon